Pebble Plus

E**X**treme
Animals

The Slowest Animals

by Catherine Ipcizade

Consulting Editor: Gail Saunders-Smith, PhD

Consultant: Tanya Dewey, PhD
University of Michigan Museum of Zoology

CAPSTONE PRESS
a capstone imprint

Pebble Plus is published by Capstone Press,
1710 Roe Crest Drive, North Mankato, Minnesota 56003.
www.capstonepub.com

Books published by Capstone Press are manufactured with paper
containing at least 10 percent post-consumer waste.

Library of Congress Cataloging-in-Publication Data
Ipcizade, Catherine.
  The slowest animals / by Catherine Ipcizade.
    p. cm. — (Pebble plus. Extreme animals)
  Includes bibliographical references and index.
  Summary: "Simple text and photographs present the world's slowest animals"—Provided by publisher.
  ISBN 978-1-4296-5310-7 (library binding)
  ISBN 978-1-4296-6209-3 (paperback)
  1. Animal locomotion—Juvenile literature. 2. Speed—Juvenile literature. I. Title.
QP301.I673 2011
591.47'9—dc22   2010028756

Editorial Credits
Katy Kudela, editor; Heidi Thompson, designer; Marcie Spence, media researcher; Laura Manthe, production specialist

Photo Credits
Ardea: Thomas Marent, 5; iStockphoto: ebettini, 7, j4r3k, 19, Jacinto Yoder, 21, JohnCarnemolla, 9, skynesher, 15;
Newscom, 11; Shutterstock: cg-art, Sinisa Botas, cover, 17, UltraOrto, S.A., 1, Vinicius Tupinamba, 13

Note to Parents and Teachers

The Extreme Animals series supports national science standards related to life science. This
book describes and illustrates animals that move slowly. The images support early readers in
understanding the text. The repetition of words and phrases helps early readers learn new
words. This book also introduces early readers to subject-specific vocabulary words, which are
defined in the Glossary section. Early readers may need assistance to read some words and to
use the Table of Contents, Glossary, Read More, Internet Sites, and Index sections of the book.

Printed in the United States of America in North Mankato, Minnesota.
122014   008658R

Table of Contents

Slow

They crawl! They float!

They inch along the ground!

These animals aren't just slow.

They take slow to the EXTREME.

The slow loris hangs upside

down for hours to stalk prey.

But this animal isn't always slow.

It quickly snatches bugs.

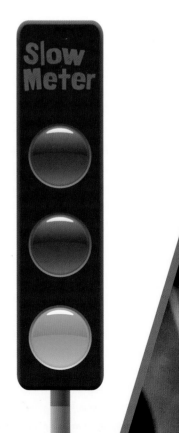

In no hurry

4

A Gila monster's legs

move slowly.

Sneaking up on prey is work.

Luckily this reptile only needs to

eat three or four times a year.

Koalas have to eat a lot of

eucalyptus leaves

to get enough nutrients.

To save energy, a koala moves

slowly and sleeps a lot.

Slower

A giant anteater moves slowly.

But it doesn't have a choice.

To keep its claws sharp,

it walks on the sides

of its front paws.

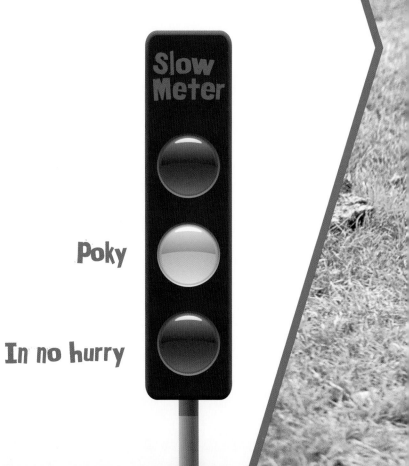

Poky

In no hurry

An earthworm makes its home

in wet, warm soil.

This dirt digger may be slow.

But its movement mixes the soil

and helps plants grow.

A sea horse wiggles

through the ocean.

It is too slow to hunt.

A sea horse just sucks in

shrimp floating by.

Slowest

How fast could you move

if you had to carry

your house on your back?

Garden snails carry their shells

wherever they go.

SLUGGISH!

Poky

In no hurry

A Galapagos tortoise is too big to move fast. This reptile can weigh up to 573 pounds (260 kilograms). That's more than two baby elephants!

A sloth might hang in

one spot all day.

This slow animal

uses its sharp claws

to hang from tree branches.

Glossary

claw—a hard, curved nail on the foot of a bird or other animal

energy—the strength to do active things without getting tired

eucalpytus—a strong-smelling evergreen tree that grows in dry places

nutrient—something that is needed by people, animals, and plants to stay strong and healthy

prey—an animal that is hunted by another animal for food

reptile—a cold-blooded animal that breathes air and has a backbone; most reptiles lay eggs and have scaly skin

soil—dirt or earth in which plants grow

stalk—to hunt or track a person or an animal in a quiet, secret way

Read More

Stockland, Patricia M. *Swing, Slither, or Swim: A Book About Animal Movement.* Animal Wise. Minneapolis: Picture Window Books, 2005.

Stout, Frankie. *Nature's Slowest Animals.* Extreme Animals. New York: PowerKids Press, 2008.

Internet Sites

FactHound offers a safe, fun way to find Internet sites related to this book. All of the sites on FactHound have been researched by our staff.

Here's all you do:

Visit *www.facthound.com*

Type in this code: 9781429653107

Check out projects, games and lots more at **www.capstonekids.com**

Index

Word Count: 231
Grade: 1
Early-Intervention Level: 18